Take the Lead!

Copyright © 2005 by Ron Kaufman.
All rights reserved. The moral right of the author has been asserted.

Published by Ron Kaufman Pte Ltd. - 10 9 8 7 6 5 4 3 2

Lift Me Up! - Take the Lead!
ISBN 981-05-2931-7 — 136 pages.

1. Leadership
2. Quotations
3. Self-Help
4. Ron Kaufman
5. Title

Cover and page layout by The Bonsey Design Partnership.
Cover illustrations by Ngu Hie Ling.
Set in Times and Arial fonts. Printed in Singapore.

Every effort has been made to credit the original author and make full acknowledgement of the source for each quotation in this text. However, if you know of any instance where the quotation or citation could be more accurate, please send a message to Ron@RonKaufman.com Any corrections will gladly be included in future editions. Thank you.

Below each attributed quotation are **quips, quotes and anecdotes in bold text**. These additional notes are by Ron Kaufman (1956 –), who should be cited as the author in all future works.

Ron Kaufman, Lift Me Up!, Pick Me Up!, UP Your Service!, and a balloon with the word *'UP'* are registered trademarks of Ron Kaufman Pte Ltd.

All rights reserved. No part of this book may be reproduced, stored, archived or transmitted in any form by mechanical or electronic means including information storage and retrieval systems without permission in writing from the publisher, except for the quotation of brief passages in book reviews.

Additional copies of this book are available at discount for promotional events, contests, awards, and in-house training programs. For details and fast delivery, contact:

Ron Kaufman Pte Ltd
50 Bayshore Park #31-01
Aquamarine Tower
Singapore 469977

Tel: (+65) 6441-2760
Fax: (+65) 6444-8292
Ron@RonKaufman.com
www.RonKaufman.com

Contents

Create a powerful vision	4
Take the first step forward	25
Your strategy is essential	67
The character of a leader	94

Create a powerful vision

The empires of the future are empires of the mind.

Winston Churchill

**Beautiful future?
Beautiful mind!**

You read a book from beginning to end. You run a business the opposite way. You start with the end, and then you do everything you must to reach it.

Harold Geneen

**Can you see the end?
That's the beginning.**

The great successful men of the world have used their imagination... they think ahead and create their mental picture in all its details, filling in here, adding a little there, altering this a bit and that a bit, but steadily building – steadily building.

Robert Collier

Use your imagination. Fill it in!

The best way to predict the future is to create it.

Peter Drucker

Here's a sure prediction: Your future is up to you.

We are told never to cross a bridge until we come to it, but this world is owned by men who have 'crossed bridges' in their imagination far ahead of the crowd.

Dale Carnegie

If you can dream it, then you can achieve it. You will get all you want in life if you help enough other people get what they want.

Zig Ziglar

Build a bridge. Then another, and another, and another...

What goes around, comes around. (You know that.)

Without vision the
people perish.

The Bible

**With *your* vision, let the
whole world flourish.**

You must first clearly
see a thing in your mind
before you can do it.

Alex Morrison

Visualization works.

Big results require big ambitions.

James Champy

How big are yours?

The starting point of all achievement is desire. Keep this constantly in mind. Weak desires bring weak results, just as a small amount of fire makes a small amount of heat.

Napoleon Hill

**Got a strong desire?
Let it light your fire!**

Ambition is so powerful a passion in the human breast, that however high we reach we are never satisfied.

Niccolò dei Machiavelli

Don't let that stop you. Keep reaching!

It is more important to know where you are going than to get there quickly.

Mabel Newcomber

Enjoy the journey, step by step.

The more clear you are on what you want, the more power you will have.

Mark Victor Hansen

An unfocused telescope cannot see the stars.

The most distinguishing feature of winners is their intensity of purpose.

Alymer Letterman

Winners *are* intense. Are you?

The men who succeed are the efficient few. They are the few who have the ambition and willpower to develop themselves.

Herbert Casson

There is no advancement to him who stands trembling because he cannot see the end from the beginning.

E.J. Klemme

You can do it. Yes – you!

Take the first step.

Success is the progressive realization of a worthy goal or ideal.

Earl Nightingale

Above all be of single aim; have a legitimate and useful purpose, and devote yourself unreservedly to it.

James Allen

Success takes time. And feels so good!

Live your life with purpose.

The reason most people never reach their goals is that they don't define them, learn about them, or even seriously consider them as believable or achievable. Winners can tell you where they are going, what they plan to do along the way, and who will be sharing the adventure with them.

Denis Waitley

Wherever you see a successful business, someone once made a courageous decision.

Peter Drucker

Thanks for sharing this adventure with me!

Be bold. Have courage. You can do it!

Your goals, minus your doubts, equal your reality.

Ralph Marston

Desire! That's the one secret of every man's career. Not education. Not being born with hidden talents. Desire.

Bobby Unser

Goals and doubts are both part of life. (But keep your goals going stronger!)

Make your desires strong – not secret.

The first principle of success is desire: knowing what you want. Desire is the planting of your seed.

Robert Collier

The best leaders continually light the way.

Marshall Thurber

Small seeds (well planted) yield great forests of achievement.

Let your light shine brightly.

Ambition can creep as well as soar.

Edmund Burke

Just keep moving.

Vision without action is merely a dream.
Action without vision just passes the time.
Vision with action can change the world.

Joel Barker

See a better world, then act to make it so.

Anticipating a new reality is the beginning of the process of creating it.

Faith Popcorn

The future belongs to those who see possibilities before they become obvious.

John Scully

What's around the corner? Peek!

Got a hunch? You've got the future.

At first people refuse to believe that a strange new thing can be done, then they begin to hope that it can be done, then they see that it can be done, then it is done and all the world wonders why it was not done centuries ago.

Frances Burnett

Don't wait for centuries. Be strange right now.

The very essence of leadership is that you have to have a vision.

Theodore Hesburgh

Sharing your vision leads people forward.

We don't ask consumers what they want. They don't know. Instead we apply our brain power to what they need, and will want, and make sure we're there, ready.

Akio Morita

What do your customers need today? What will they want tomorrow? Are you ready?

Singleness of purpose is one of the chief essentials for success in life, no matter what may be one's aim.

John D. Rockefeller, Jr.

Aim true. Aim high.

When you reach for the stars, you may not quite get one, but you won't come up with a handful of mud either.

Leo Burnett

Imagination is more important than knowledge.

Albert Einstein

Aim higher than you can reach.

Imagine that!

I dream for a living.

Steven Spielberg

You are today where your thoughts have brought you; you will be tomorrow where your thoughts take you.

James Allen

Everyone dreams at night. Creative genius dreams all day.

Taking charge of your thoughts takes charge of your tomorrow.

The intuitive mind is a sacred gift, and the rational mind is a faithful servant. We have created a society that honors the servant and has forgotten the gift.

Albert Einstein

Let your rational abilities be guided by your sacred intuition.

The greatest danger for most of us is not that our aim is too high and we miss it, but that our aim is too low and we reach it.

Michelangelo

Shoot for the moon. Even if you miss, you'll be among the stars.

You've got to think about big things while you're doing small things, so that all the small things go in the right direction.

Alvin Toffler

Great minds have purposes, others have wishes.

Washington Irving

Imagine the garden while you are planting the seeds.

**Be powerful.
Be on purpose.**

Take the first step forward

Leadership is the art of getting someone else to do something you want done because he wants to do it.

Dwight Eisenhower

Leadership is the capacity to translate vision into reality.

Warren Bennis

Give other people what they want, and they will help you get what you want.

Be a translator. Speak up!

Surround yourself with the best people you can find, delegate authority, and don't interfere.

Ronald Reagan

When placed in command – take charge.

Norman Schwarzkopf

An orchestral conductor reads the score, but does not play the music.

Your team is counting on you.

If I have seen farther than other men it is by standing on the shoulders of giants.

Isaac Newton

Take the wisdom of others, and then take it further.

Management is efficiency in climbing the ladder of success; leadership determines whether the ladder is leaning against the right wall.

Stephen Covey

Climbing fast doesn't help if you get to the wrong destination.

A leader is a dealer in hope.

Napoleon Bonaparte

Be a vendor of optimism, possibilities and power.

Commitment is what transforms a promise into reality.

Abraham Lincoln

Keep your promises.

If one advances confidently in the direction of his dreams, and endeavors to live the life which he has imagined, he will meet with a success unexpected in common hours.

Henry David Thoreau

Let your life be uncommonly good.

Be willing to make decisions. That's the most important quality in a good leader. Don't fall victim to what I call the ready-aim-aim-aim-aim syndrome. You must be willing to fire.

T. Boone Pickens

Don't sit on important questions too long. Make a decision.

The ultimate leader is one who is willing to develop people to the point that they eventually surpass him or her in knowledge and ability.

Fred Manske, Jr.

If you tell people where to go, but not how to get there, you'll be amazed at the results.

George Patton

The greatest teachers have students who become even better teachers.

You explain why. Let them figure out how.

A leader knows what's best to do; a manager knows how best to do it.

Ken Adelman

You need both to get the right job done right.

You don't manage people; you manage things. You lead people.

Grace Hooper

Pallets? Reach for trucks and forklifts. People? Reach for hearts and minds.

Outstanding leaders appeal to the hearts of their followers.

Nelson Mandela

Let people *feel* your commitment.

Management works in the system. Leadership works on the system.

Stephen Covey

Know when to manage and when to lead.

A leader's role is to raise people's aspirations for what they can become – and to release their energies so they will strive to get there.

David Gergen

Leaders must be close enough to relate to others, but far enough ahead to motivate them.

John Maxwell

Raise their sights. Help release their passion.

Look forward to see where you are going. Reach back to bring your team along.

A leader takes people where they want to go. A great leader takes people where they don't necessarily want to go, but ought to be.

Rosalynn Carter

Catch someone doing something right.

Kenneth Blanchard & Spencer Johnson

Have the conviction to take them higher.

Forget 'Employee of the Month'. Recognize your best 'Employees of the Moment!'

People underestimate their capacity for change. There is never a right time to do a difficult thing. A leader's job is to help people have vision of their potential.

John Porter

If you want people to listen, you have to have a platform to speak from, and that is excellence in all you do.

Bill Pollard

Be a mirror in which others fall in love with their potential.

You must earn the platform. Be a model of excellence in your life.

A good manager is a man who isn't worried about his own career but rather the careers of those who work for him. My advice: don't worry about yourself. Take care of those who work for you and you'll float to greatness on their achievements.

H.S.M. Burns

When your team does a good job, you've done a good job.

Let us not look back in anger or forward in fear, but around in awareness.

James Thurber

Your life arises in every present moment. Be right here, right now.

A leader is one who knows the way, goes the way and shows the way.

John Maxwell

You are the way ahead for those who follow.

Pay heed to nourishing the troops. Do not unnecessarily fatigue them. Unite them in spirit.

Sun Tzu

Life is more than work. Throw a party!

Review your goals twice every day in order to be focused on achieving them.

Les Brown

Plan your progress carefully; hour by hour, day by day, month by month. Organized activity and maintained enthusiasm are the wellsprings of your power.

Paul Meyer

When you wake, what do you want to achieve today? When you go to sleep, what do you want to achieve tomorrow?

First plan your work. Then work your plan.

The quality of expectations determines the quality of our action.

Andre Godin

Expect the best, plan for the worst, and prepare to be surprised.

Denis Waitley

Have huge expectations of yourself and others. Huge action and results will follow.

Luck favors the prepared mind.

The first task of a leader is to keep hope alive.

Joe Batten

The first responsibility of a leader is to define reality. The last is to say thank you. In between, the leader is a servant.

Max De Pree

Nourish your hopes and dreams. Let them be contagious.

How may I help you?

Alliances make an army strong.

Sun Tzu

Behind every able man, there are always other able men.

Chinese proverb

Join hands. Team up. Work together.

No one succeeds in this life all alone.

A total commitment is paramount to reaching ultimate performance.

Tom Flores

These four words make the difference: 'I am totally committed.'

Strong beliefs win strong men, and then make them stronger.

Walter Bagehot

What do you believe most strongly?

It does not take much strength to do things, but it requires great strength to decide what to do.

Chow Ching

A decision without the pressure of consequence is hardly a decision at all.

Eric Langmuir

**Build your strength.
Decide what to do.
Decide what not to do.**

**What consequences arose from your recent decisions?
What consequences will come from the decisions you are about to make?**

It is better to be boldly decisive and risk being wrong than to agonize at length and be right, but too late.

Marilyn Kennedy

If you don't risk anything, you risk even more.

Erica Jong

A bad decision on Monday is better than a good decision on Friday. You'll have all week to make corrections.

Take the risk of doing something new.

Leadership is getting someone to do what they don't want to do, to achieve what they want to achieve.

Tom Landry

You have to perform at a consistently higher level than others. That's the mark of a true professional.

Joe Paterno

People can tolerate any 'how' if you give them a big enough 'why'. Show them a very big 'why'.

**Raise your standards.
Raise your sights.
Raise the bar.**

The speed of the leader determines the rate of the pack.

Wayne Lukas

When you are the one in front, race like the wind!

Hold yourself responsible for a higher standard than anybody else expects of you. Never excuse yourself. Never pity yourself. Be a hard master to yourself and be lenient to everybody else.

Henry Ward Beecher

Set an example. Be an example. Don't make an example of anyone else.

High achievement always takes place in the framework of high expectation.

Jack Kinder

High expectations are the key to everything.

Sam Walton

Stretch your own expectations.

Whatever you expect of yourself now, make it bigger, higher, bolder. Be more outstanding.

Nothing can add more power to your life than concentrating all your energies on a limited set of targets.

Nido Qubein

Choose one or two, three or four. Not thirty.

Fame usually comes to those who are thinking about something else.

Oliver Wendell Holmes

Serving others is the primary aim. Fame and profit are the applause.

The weakest creature, by concentrating his power on a single object, can accomplish good results; while the strongest, by dispersing his effort over many chores, may fail to accomplish anything. Drops of water, by continually falling, hone their passage through the hardest of rocks, but the hasty torrent rushes over it and leaves no trace behind.

Og Mandino

Concentration = Power

Define your dream, and then build your team.

Mark Victor Hansen & Jack Canfield

Mark and Jack created *Chicken Soup for the Soul*. Millions of copies sold, and millions of dollars given to charity. What's *your* dream? Who's on *your* team?

The successful man is the average man, focused.

Wayne Dyer

If you chase two rabbits, you will catch neither.

Iain Batey

Are you average today? Want to be more successful tomorrow? Step One: get more focused – right now.

Ever try running right and left at the same time? Doesn't work. Choose one direction.

The shortest way to do many things is to do only one thing at a time.

Sydney Smiles

...and do that one thing extremely well.

Motivation is everything. You can do the work of two people, but you can't be two people. Instead, you have to inspire the next guy down the line and get him to inspire his people.

Lee Iacocca

Take the action that encourages new action. Start a chain reaction.

It is the responsibility of leadership to provide opportunity, and the responsibility of individuals to contribute.

Bill Pollard

Rank does not confer privilege or give power. It imposes responsibility.

Peter Drucker

Feed your team big opportunities.

Getting promoted means climbing the ladder of responsibility. The higher you go, the more weight you carry.

The ability to accept responsibility is the measure of the man.

Roy Hunt

You can only govern men by serving them.

Victor Cousin

How much can you handle? How much are you willing to bear?

Bosses serve their staff. Leaders serve their teams. Partners serve each other.

Never look down on anybody unless you're helping him up.

Jesse Jackson

Success is not counted by how high you have climbed but by how many people you brought with you.

Wil Rose

Extend your hand to those who need the help. As they rise, so will you.

How many people have you brought to greater heights?

You train people how to treat you by how you treat yourself.

Martin Rutte

Treat yourself as somebody special.

There are many elements to a campaign. Leadership is number one. Everything else is number two.

Bertolt Brecht

Get your leadership right and everything else will follow.

Having once decided to achieve a certain task, achieve it at all costs of tedium and distaste. The gain in self-confidence of having accomplished a tiresome labor is immense.

Thomas Bennett

Do the hard things first.

Not the cry, but the flight of the wild duck, leads the flock to fly and follow.

Chinese proverb

Don't just quack. Soar!

Tell everyone what you want to do and someone will want to help you do it.

W. Clement Stone

Tell the world your dreams and the world will help you reach them.

He who does too much often does too little.

Italian proverb

Don't let being busy keep you from doing something worthy.

No man will make a great leader who wants to do it all himself or get all the credit for doing it.

Andrew Carnegie

Pass out purpose, projects and praise!

It is not work that kills men; it is worry. Worry is rust upon the blade.

Henry Ward Beecher

What's got you worried? Go to work on it instead.

The final test of a leader is that he leaves behind him in others the conviction and will to carry on.

Walter Lippmann

If you help others, you will be helped. Perhaps tomorrow, perhaps in a hundred years, but you will be helped. Nature must pay off the debt.

Georges Gurdjieff

How will your team perform after you are gone?

What goes around, comes around. What you send out, comes back. It's the way of the world.

Lead, follow or get out of the way.

Ted Turner

If you have built castles in the air, your work need not be lost; that is where they should be. Now put the foundations under them.

Henry David Thoreau

If you lead, do it strongly. If you follow, do it passionately. If you get out of the way, *stay* out of the way. Now, choose your position.

A lofty vision calls for earthly action.

The art of leadership is saying no, not yes. It is very easy to say yes.

Tony Blair

The hero is one who kindles a great light in the world, who sets up blazing torches in the dark streets of life for other people to see by.

Felix Adler

Difficult choices are the test of your leadership. Welcome them when they come.

Where there is sadness, bring joy. Where there is darkness, bring light.

To truly get anywhere, you must first find courage to lose sight of the familiar shore.

Johann Wolfgang von Goethe

Standing in the middle of the road is very dangerous; you get knocked down by traffic from both sides.

Margaret Thatcher

Great destinations are over the horizon.

Choose a clear direction. Going both ways gets you nowhere.

If we took the mission statements of 100 large industrial companies, mixed them up while everyone was asleep, and reassigned them at random, would anyone wake up tomorrow and cry, 'My gosh, where has our mission statement gone?'

Gary Hamel

Leaders keep their eyes on the horizon, not just the bottom line.

Warren Bennis

Do you have a unique and powerful mission? What is it?

The big bottom line is well over the horizon. Look out, not down.

If we listened to our intellect, we'd never have a love affair. We'd never have a friendship. We'd never go into business, because we'd be cynical. Well, that's nonsense. You've got to jump off cliffs all the time and build your wings on the way down.

Ray Bradbury

It's always worthwhile to make others aware of their worth.

Malcolm Forbes

Parachutes open after you jump. Wings only work when you're flying.

Other people see their worth reflected in your eyes. Show them a beautiful picture.

The finest gift you can give is encouragement. Yet almost no one gets the encouragement they need to grow to their full potential. If everyone received the encouragement they need to grow, genius would blossom and produce abundance beyond our dreams.

Sidney Madwed

Encourage at least one new person every day. Appreciate those who truly encourage you.

Our heads are round to permit our thoughts to change direction.

Lars Wallentin

Don't get stuck thinking only one way!

There's nothing you can't accomplish if you clearly decide what you're absolutely committed to achieving, you're willing to take massive action, you notice what's working or not, and you change your approach until you achieve what you want, using whatever life gives along the way.

Anthony Robbins

When you give a lot to life, life gives a lot to you.

As long as you're going to be thinking anyway, THINK BIG.

Donald Trump

Your imagination is elastic. Stretch!

Risk more than others think is safe. Care more than others think is wise. Dream more than others think is practical. Expect more than others think is possible.

Army Cadet maxim

Concentrate your strengths against your competitor's relative weaknesses.

Bruce Henderson

Take the high road.

Grow where there is space for you to flourish.

An unpolished plan vigorously executed is more successful than an ideal plan implemented with less determination. Better to strike energetically, gain experience, learn what works and what does not, reassess the new situation, devise fresh plans and take another step. Spend too long preparing elaborate plans, and you will lose both time and initiative.

Lee Hsien Loong

Don't wait. Strike while the iron is hot.

When you cannot make up your mind which of two evenly balanced courses of action you should take – choose the bolder.

William Joseph Slim

Have courage. Be bold! Fortune favors the brave.

A conclusion is the place where you got tired of thinking.

Junah Sowojay Boda

Think it all the way through.

Who dares, wins.

Ian Fleming

Take the plunge.

Nothing focuses the mind better than the constant sight of a competitor who wants to wipe you off the map.

Wayne Calloway

Small opportunities are often the beginning of great enterprises.

Demosthenes

Competition is like cod liver oil. First it makes you sick. Then it makes you better.

Start with a seed to grow a great tree.

A journey of a thousand miles must begin with a single step.

Lao-tzu

Take a step in the direction of your dreams.

To begin is the most important part of any quest, and by far the most courageous.

Plato

Begin right now!

If you have an important point to make, don't try to be subtle or clever. Use the pile driver. Hit the point once. Then come back and hit it again. Then hit it a third time; a tremendous whack.

Winston Churchill

Leadership involves finding a parade and getting in front of it.

John Naisbitt

People can be thick. Drive your point home!

Then guiding that parade in the best direction.

Leadership and learning are indispensable to each other.

John F. Kennedy

To be an expert in your field, read deeply inside your niche. To become innovative, read widely outside your niche.

Jeff Bezos

Leaders are learning all their lives. Are you?

Visit a library, a bookstore, a new website. Keep reading!

Nothing will ever be attempted if all possible objections must first be overcome.

Samuel Johnson

It's not the plan that is important, it's the planning.

Graeme Edwards

You cannot know everything before you start. Get started knowing what you know.

Plans are rarely what happens. Planning ensures something happens.

You can't run a business without taking risks.

Millard Drexler

Learn the difference between risks that can teach you and risks that can destroy you.

No one reaches a high position without daring.

Publilius Syrus

Attempt something you think may – or may not – succeed.

Entrepreneurs are risk takers, willing to roll the dice with their money or reputation on the line in support of an idea or enterprise. They willingly assume responsibility for the success or failure of a venture and are answerable for all its facets. The buck not only stops at their desks, it starts there too.

Victor Kiam

Select an enterprise or an idea you believe in, and get rolling.

Why wait? Life is not a dress rehearsal. Quit practising what you're going to do, and just do it. In one bold stroke you can transform today.

Marilyn Grey

Just do it – today!

Compromise is the art of dividing a cake in such a way that everyone believes he has the biggest piece.

Ludwig Erhard

Time is the scarcest resource. Unless time is managed, nothing else can be managed.

Peter Drucker

Work it out so that everyone is a winner.

The bad news is time flies. The good news is you are the pilot.

Entrepreneurs are those who understand there is little difference between obstacle and opportunity and are able to turn both to their advantage.

Victor Kiam

Obstacles are merely opportunities in work clothes.

You cannot build a great reputation on what you say you are going to do.

John Rockefeller, Sr.

You build a reputation by what you actually do.

Do not despise the bottom rungs in the ascent to greatness.

Publilius Syrus

Tall buildings need deep foundations. Dig in.

Two important things I did learn: you are as powerful and strong as you allow yourself to be, and the most difficult part of any endeavor is taking the first step, making the first decision.

Robyn Davidson

Aim high and get started.

The first man gets the oyster, the second man gets the shell.

Andrew Carnegie

Learn from the past, set vivid, detailed goals for the future, and live in the only moment of time over which you have any control: now.

Denis Waitley

Earn and enjoy the first-mover advantage.

This moment is full of magic and power and grace. That's why we call it 'the present'.

Give whatever you are doing and whoever you are with the gift of your full attention.

Jim Rohn

When you write down your ideas you automatically focus your full attention on them. Few if any of us can write one thought and think another at the same time. A pencil and paper make excellent tools for concentration.

Michael Leboeuf

Embrace the miracle of each moment.

Put pen and paper in your pocket, by your bed and in your hands.

If you stop learning today, you stop leading tomorrow.

Howard Hendricks

Today a reader – tomorrow a leader.

W. Fusselman

The world is constantly changing. To stay in front, you must keep changing, too.

Knowledge is power.

Excellence is a better teacher than mediocrity. Lessons of the ordinary are everywhere. Truly profound and original insights are to be found only in studying the exemplary.

Warren Bennis

An entrepreneur tends to bite off a little more than he can chew hoping he'll quickly learn how to chew it.

Roy Ash

Who is exemplary in your business? In your industry? In your life?

Open wide and bite!

The roads we take are more important than the goals we announce.

Frederick Speakman

Well-arranged time is the surest mark of a well-arranged mind.

Judith Pitman

Enjoy your journey – all the way.

Plan time on, and time off.

Life is like a dogsled team. If you ain't the lead dog, the scenery never changes.

Lewis Grizzard

Put yourself in the lead of your own life.

Often a certain abdication of prudence and foresight is an element of success.

Ralph Waldo Emerson

Sometimes you must take a step of faith.

Life is like a hand of cards. You have to play the hand you're dealt, you can't win by folding, and sometimes you must take chances in order to win.

Mike Conner

The wise man bridges the gap by laying out a path by means of which he can get from where he is to where he wants to go.

John Pierpont Morgan

Do the best you can with what you've got.

Choose a place worth going to, then make a plan to get there.

Success covers many blunders.

George Bernard Shaw

Racing is a matter of spirit not strength.

Janet Guthrie

Celebrate triumphs. Remember tribulations.

You must have the will to win.

The wise man always throws himself on the side of his assailants. It is more in his own interest than in theirs to find his weak point.

Ralph Waldo Emerson

The toughest part of getting to the top of the ladder is getting through the crowd at the bottom.

Jack Nicklaus

When you find it, fix it.

Move up. Reach high. Stand out!

Never give in – never, never, never, never, in nothing great or small, large or petty, never give in except to convictions of honor and good sense. Never yield to force; never yield to the apparently overwhelming might of the enemy.

Winston Churchill

'Giving up' is not an option.

It has always seemed to me that your brand is formed primarily not by what your company says about itself, but what the company does.

Jeff Bezos

**What do you say?
What do you do?
Is there a difference?**

The victorious strategist only seeks battle after the victory has been won, whereas he who is destined to defeat first fights and afterwards looks for victory.

Sun Tzu

If each of us hires people who are smaller than we are, we shall become a company of dwarfs. But if each of us hires people who are bigger than we are, we shall become a company of giants.

David Ogilvy

**Strategy first.
Battle later.**

Surround yourself with giants.

The ability to learn faster than your competitors may be the only sustainable competitive advantage.

Arie De Geus

Good tactics can save even the worst strategy. Bad tactics will destroy even the best strategy.

George Patton

How much faster can you learn?

Strategy is the big picture, and is essential. Tactics are the brush strokes, and each can be decisive.

The character of a leader

Character is like a tree and reputation like a shadow. The shadow is what we think of it; the tree is the real thing.

Abraham Lincoln

The people I look for to fill top management spots are the eager beavers, the mavericks. These are the people who try to do more than they're expected to do – they always reach.

Lee Iacocca

Focus on character. Reputation follows.

Are you an eager beaver or a meandering moose?

The price of greatness is responsibility.

Winston Churchill

The measure of a man's character is what he would do if he knew he would never be found out.

Baron Thomas

How much responsibility are you willing to carry?

Don't cheat. Don't lie. You have to live with yourself.

Four short words sum up what has lifted most successful individuals above the crowd: a little bit more. They did all that was expected of them and a little bit more.

Lou Vickery

The five essential entrepreneurial skills for success: concentration, discrimination, organization, innovation and communication.

Michael Gerber

How can you do a little more?

And getting the five to work together is six.

The heights by great men reached and kept, were not attained by sudden flight. But they, while their companions slept, were toiling upward in the night.

Henry Wadsworth Longfellow

A man who is at the top has a habit of getting to the bottom.

Joseph Rogers

Buy some midnight oil and burn it.

To climb a tall ladder, make sure it is steady at the bottom.

Make yourself indispensable and you will move up. Act as though you are indispensable and you will get moved out.

Jules Ormont

Be useful. Keep quiet. Move ahead.

The test of a first-rate intelligence is the ability to hold two opposed ideas in the mind at the same time, and still retain the ability to function.

F. Scott Fitzgerald

Match your best ideas with their contradictions. What makes sense?

The purpose of life is not to win. The purpose of life is to grow and to share. When you come to look back on all that you have done in life, you will get more satisfaction from the pleasure you have brought into other people's lives than you will from the times that you outdid and defeated them.

Harold Kushner

Help someone else succeed today.

You have to have your heart in the business and the business in your heart.

Thomas Watson

Pour your heart into what you do and what you do will fill your heart.

A successful career will no longer be about promotion. It will be about mastery.

Michael Hammer

The will to win, the desire to succeed, the urge to reach your full potential. These are the keys that will unlock the door to personal excellence.

Eddie Robinson

Promote mastery in your organization.

You've got the keys in your hands. Use them!

One person with a belief is equal to a force of ninety-nine who have only interests.

John Stuart Mill

Someone who sees leadership as a means for his own personal gain does not have the credentials to be a leader.

Kim Woo-Chong

Hire those who believe, not those who are just interested.

Look beyond yourself. The greatest gains lie in serving others.

If you have knowledge, let others light their candles with it.

Winston Churchill

Sharing lights up the world.

No great man ever complains of want of opportunity.

Ralph Waldo Emerson

Great people create opportunities, not complaints.

No horse gets anywhere until he is harnessed. No stream or gas drives anything until it is confined. No life ever grows great until it is focused, dedicated, disciplined.

Harry Emerson Fosdick

Nearly all men can stand adversity, but if you want to test a man's character, give him power.

Abraham Lincoln

Focus increases your power.

As your power grows, will you use it wisely?

In reading the lives of great men, I found that the first victory they won was over themselves. With all of them, self-discipline came first.

Harry Truman

Regardless of how you feel inside, always try to look like a winner. Even if you are behind, a sustained look of control and confidence can give you a mental edge that results in victory.

Arthur Ashe

Harness your potential. A horse running wild wins no races.

See yourself victorious.

Success gravitates toward those who are perceived to be successful. Regardless of how you feel within, you must emanate success if you want to attract people to your cause.

Jeff Herman

Nurture your mind with great thoughts, for you will never go any higher than you think.

Benjamin Disraeli

Ask your mirror on the wall: 'Do I look like a success at all?'

Read autobiographies of people you admire. One day, others may read yours.

All the extraordinary men I have known were extraordinary in their own estimation.

Woodrow Wilson

Believe in yourself. You *are* extraordinary.

Quality questions create a quality life. Successful people ask better questions, and as a result, they get better answers.

Anthony Robbins

What is the best question you asked today? What is the best question someone else asked you?

The boss drives people; the leader coaches them. The boss depends on authority; the leader on goodwill. The boss inspires fear. The leader inspires enthusiasm. The boss says 'I'. The leader says 'We'. The boss fixes the blame for the breakdown. The leader helps fix the breakdown. The boss says 'Go'. The leader says 'Let's go!'

Gordon Selfridge

Be a leader, not a boss.

When you appeal to the highest level of thinking, you get the highest level of performance.

Jack Stack

Bold thinking leads to bold results.

When the work of a great leader is done, and his aim is fulfilled, the people will say 'We did it ourselves.'

Lao-tzu

You cannot dream yourself into a character; you must hammer and forge yourself one.

James Froude

A true leader will agree, praise and smile.

It takes hard work – and a few hard knocks.

A boss creates fear, a leader confidence. A boss fixes blame, a leader corrects mistakes. A boss knows all, a leader asks questions. A boss makes work drudgery, a leader makes it interesting. A boss is interested in himself or herself, a leader is interested in the group.

Russell Ewing

Ordinary men hate solitude. But the Master makes use of it, embracing his aloneness, realizing he is one with the whole universe.

Lao-tzu

Fire the boss. Promote the leader – in you.

Enjoy some peace and quiet.

A great man is always willing to be little.

Ralph Waldo Emerson

Be humble in your hour of greatest triumph.

When you have a plan, you are more comfortable. When you are prepared, you are more confident.

Fred Couples

**Be comfortable – plan.
Be confident – prepare.**

Optimism is the faith that leads to achievement. Nothing can be done without hope and confidence.

Helen Keller

Winning breeds confidence and confidence breeds winning.

Hubert Green

She was blind, deaf and learned to speak, but she had optimism, hope and faith. You can see, hear and speak. What else have you got?

Pick one 'win' you achieved today, large or small. Good for you! (Now create another.)

With confidence, you can reach truly amazing heights; without confidence, even simple accomplishments are beyond your grasp.

Jim Loehr

Self-confidence is the first requisite to great undertakings.

Samuel Johnson

Your first accomplishment must be believing in yourself.

If you can dream it, you can do it.

Experience tells you what to do; confidence allows you to do it.

Stan Smith

It's nice to be important, but it's more important to be nice.

John Cassis

**Try more.
Do more.
Grow more.**

Give a smile and a compliment to each person you see today.

I honestly believed I would make it. I had the desire. A lot of people have the ability, but they don't put forth the effort.

Joe Carter

Effort sets you apart from others.

The elevator to success is out of order. You'll have to use the stairs... one step at a time.

Joe Girard

And the view from the top is so sweet.

We all have ability. The difference is how we use it.

Stevie Wonder

Put yours to work!

I can't imagine a person becoming a success who doesn't give this game of life everything he's got.

Walter Cronkite

Play life to the fullest.

There is a real magic in enthusiasm. It spells the difference between mediocrity and accomplishment.

Norman Vincent Peale

Enthusiasm is best spelled Y-E-S.

Wear your learning, like your watch, in a private pocket. Do not pull it out and strike it merely to show that you have one.

Earl of Chesterfield

Keep your education quiet. Let your results speak most clearly.

If you let your head get too big, it'll break your neck.

Elvis Presley

A man cannot govern a nation if he cannot govern a city; he cannot govern a city if he cannot govern a family; he cannot govern a family unless he can govern himself; and he cannot govern himself unless his passions are subject to reason.

Hugo Grotius

Humility helps. It keeps your head on straight.

Control yourself.

Negotiations are a rough game, but never let them become a dirty game. Once you agree, don't back out unless the other party fails to deliver. Your handshake is your bond. As an entrepreneur, a reputation for integrity is your most valuable commodity. If you try to put something over on someone, it will come back to haunt you.

Victor Kiam

When you say it, mean it.

Don't compromise yourself. It's all you've got.

Janis Joplin

Stand up for what you believe, what you want and who you are.

The key to everything is patience. You get the chicken by hatching the egg, not by smashing it.

Arnold Glasgow

Life shrinks or expands in proportion to one's courage.

Anaïs Nin

You enjoy hot coffee and fine wine in sips, not gulps. Take your time.

**Be brave.
Live a bigger life.**

During a very busy life I have often been asked, 'How did you manage to do it all?' The answer is very simple. I did everything promptly.

Richard Tangye

Success comes to the person who does today what you were thinking about doing tomorrow.

Atul Mathur

Procrastination saps your strength. Action builds your power.

Do it now.

I've found that luck is quite predictable. If you want more luck, take more chances. Be more active. Show up more often.

Brian Tracy

Self-image sets the boundaries of individual accomplishment.

Maxwell Maltz

A hole in one only comes to the golfer who plays.

Expand your boundaries.

Self-esteem is the reputation we acquire within ourselves.

Nathaniel Branden

Become the most worthwhile person you know.

Value your listening and reading time at roughly ten times your talking time. This will assure you that you are on a course of continuous learning and self-improvement.

Gerald McGinnis

You have two ears to hear and two eyes to see, but only one mouth to speak.

There is no challenge more challenging than the challenge to improve yourself.

Michael Staley

Take the greatest challenge.

No one ever excused his way to success.

Dave Del Dotto

Don't make or take excuses.

Don't wait for someone to take you under their wing. Find a good wing and climb underneath it.

Frank Bucaro

Find a high-flying mentor.

A wise man turns chance into good fortune.

Thomas Fuller

Good luck!

Success is not to be pursued; it is to be attracted by the person you become.

Jim Rohn

Analyzing what you haven't got, as well as what you have, is necessary for a successful career.

Grace Moore

Become a person who earns success.

Learn as much from your mistakes as your successes.

I want to work with the top people, because only they have the courage and the confidence and the risk-seeking profile that you need.

Laurel Cutler

There is plenty of room at the top – but no place to sit down.

Michael Jordan

Have courage. Build confidence. Take risks.

If you want to stay on top, keep climbing.

Those who know how to win are more common than those who make proper use of their victories.

Polybius

Success is not a doorway, it's a staircase.

Dottie Walters

Use your victories as stepping stones for greater contribution.

The staircase goes both ways. Climb up!

The road to success is lined with many tempting parking spaces.

Mario Andretti

Leave the parking spaces for others. Keep driving!

If you're not big enough to lose, you're not big enough to win.

Walter Reuther

Losing is part of the game. Keep playing.

You can't cross a chasm with two small steps.

Robert Schuller

He who has great power should use it lightly.

Seneca

You cannot tiptoe at the edge of hope. Take a leap of faith.

How you make use of power reveals who you are.

You should be sensitive to what your followers think. But if you just do exactly what they want, then you're not a leader.

Mahathir Mohamad

Follow effective action with quiet reflection. From the quiet reflection will come even more effective action.

Peter Drucker

Lead people where they need to go, not just where they want to go.

**High tide, low tide.
Inhale, exhale.
Action, reflection.**

Beware of endeavoring to become a great man in a hurry. One such attempt in ten thousand may succeed. These are fearful odds.

Benjamin Disraeli

The only person you are destined to become is the person you decide to be.

Ralph Waldo Emerson

**Take your time.
Step by step.**

It really *is* up to you.

We are what we
repeatedly do.
Excellence, then, is not
an act, but a habit.

Aristotle

**Cultivate excellent
habits.**

Be what you is, cuz if
you be what you ain't,
then you ain't what
you is.

Gravemarker
Boothill Cemetery
Tombstone, Arizona

**It's your life to live.
Be who you really are.**

Reason and judgement are qualities of a leader.

Tacitus

Think small and act small, and we'll get bigger. Think big and act big, and we'll get smaller.

Herb Kelleher

What is the best reason for you to lead?

Herb Kelleher launched Southwest Airlines. Started small, grew big. What are you launching?

You cannot depend on your eyes when your imagination is out of focus.

Mark Twain

A mind all logic is like a knife all blade. It makes the hand bleed that uses it.

Rabindranath Tagore

Achievements in your world begin as pictures in your mind.

Logic and imagination work well together.

Thank you for choosing, reading and sharing this book. With 512 positive tips and quips, this one is my favorite:

> The hero is one who kindles a great light in the world, who sets up blazing torches in the dark streets of life for other people to see by.
> – Felix Adler

Which is your favorite quote? Whose life will you light up with a smile or a good word today?

Wishing you a life that blazes with joy!

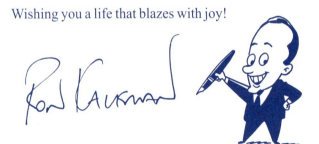

To order more copies of the **Lift Me Up!**® books, visit your local bookstore or www.LiftMeUpBooks.com